Understanding WordPress 6.x for Beginners

TIM TROTT

TIM TROTT

Contents

Preface

In "Understanding WordPress 6.x for Beginners," web designer and Tim Trott brings his three decades of experience, providing an indispensable guide for novices delving into the world of WordPress.

Unveiling the power of this ubiquitous content management system, Trott takes readers on a journey through the key functions of the WordPress dashboard. From crafting blog posts to constructing web pages, from managing media files to choosing themes that fit your vision, this comprehensive manual helps the reader through the fundamentals of the WordPress toolbox.

The author unravels the complexities of managing users and guides the user through the selection of plugin functions. Whether you need to enhance your website's functionality, improve user experience, or optimize your online presence, the guidance of this book will help you leverage the potential of WordPress.

Through practical step-by-step instructions and insights gained from teaching WordPress hands-on to customer, Tim Trott provides beginners with the knowledge and confidence needed to navigate the WordPress landscape. As you venture into this resource, you'll unlock the tools you need to create an online presence tailored to your own vision.

"Understanding WordPress 6.x for Beginners" is a useful companion for anyone embarking on their first WordPress journey, overcoming fear, and achieving success by mastering this powerful platform and realizing their creative potential.

Chapter 1

Introduction to WordPress 6.x

WordPress is an open-source content management system (CMS) that enables users to create and manage websites with no knowledge of coding or programming. It is an excellent platform for bloggers, small businesses, and entrepreneurs to publish content online and manage website data. WordPress 6.x, which includes several updates and new features. In this ebook, we will guide you through the WordPress 6.x features and how to use them to create your successful website.

WordPress is one of the most popular content management systems (CMS). It is an open-source software designed to create, manage, and publish content on websites with ease. Since its inception in 2003, WordPress has evolved into a full-blown CMS that powers over 40% of the internet. Major websites using WordPress include The Walt-Disney Company, Sony Music, Time Inc., The Rolling Stones, Mercedes-Benz, The New Yorker, BBC America, Microsoft News Center and last, but not least, The White House.

Other popular CMS platforms include Drupal and Joomla. Many common "Sitebuilders" are proprietary, which means they are locked to a particular provider, like WIX or GoDaddy.

WordPress, on the other hand, is easily transferred from one WordPress host to another.

For a beginner or an experienced website developer, WordPress provides a user-friendly platform to create websites and web applications. It is often referred to as a versatile platform because it can support a variety of websites, including blogs, e-commerce sites, and enterprise-level websites.

We will provide you with a comprehensive guide for WordPress 6.x and its features. We will cover everything from installation to advanced features that will help you take your website to the next level.

The number of functions and options may seem intimidating at first, but once you get inside, you will find many features you are familiar with already. By now, everybody has used a word processor like Microsoft Word or Apple's Pages. You'll be greeted by the familiar function "ribbon" with options for Bold, Italics, paragraph alignment, attachments and so on. We will delve into that in more detail later on.

You might wonder what, if any websites still run on the old HTML. There are a few holdouts, notably including GRC.com. HTML is not dead, however, because HTML code is what is generated by most of the Content Management System software.

The History of WordPress

WordPress was created in 2003 by Matt Mullenweg and Mike Little. It began as a fork of a blogging platform and offered users a way to create and manage their blogs.

The first public release of WordPress (version 0.7) was made available in May 2003. The platform was received positively by the online community, prompting the release of version 1.0 in January 2004.

Over the years, WordPress has undergone significant changes, both in terms of the platform's functionality and scope of its user base. In 2005, the platform introduced templates and themes, enabling users to customize their sites more easily.

In 2007, WordPress.com was launched, allowing users to create and manage their websites without having to host them independently. This brought the platform to a much broader audience, making it accessible to individual bloggers and small businesses.

In 2008, WordPress added the ability to manage multiple sites from a single installation. This was a game-changer, making managing multiple websites much more straightforward and efficient.

In 2010, WordPress introduced custom post types, allowing users to create new types of content beyond just standard blog posts. This made the platform more flexible, and businesses could now use it to create online stores, news sites, and other unique websites.

Introducing Gutenberg blocks in 2018 was a significant change. It allowed users to create more visually pleasing and interactive content forms, including easy insertion of columns and video.

Today, WordPress is the most popular website builder in the world, with over 40% of the internet powered by the platform. A commitment to accessibility, open-source development, and inclusivity has made it a vital player in the web development industry.

What is WordPress?

WordPress is a computer program. That computer program runs on a computer (the "server") which is connected to the Internet. Inside that program is a database (MySQL),, which is where all the text and data are stored. That data tells WordPress where the images are (media) and what the text is (content). The analogy that can be used here is a store mannequin.

Let's pretend that you have just been hired to work in the WordPress store. The manager points to a naked mannequin. That mannequin is your WordPress database. You can "dress it up" with any outfit you like. Let's say you want it to be a tennis player. The clothing is the Theme. You want to accessorize this mannequin, so you attach a tennis racket. The tennis racket is a Plugin. In a different season, you can change the outfit to a baseball uniform and switch the tennis racket to a baseball glove and add a baseball bat to the other hand.

Get the picture?

To continue the analogy, the WordPress store is the Server, where the mannequin "lives", but the mannequin can be moved to another "store" or Server. It's just a bit more complicated than picking up the mannequin and taking it out the door and down the street.

Chapter 2

Getting started with WordPress 6.x

When it comes to content management systems (CMS), WordPress is the most popular one in the world. It powers around 39% of all websites on the internet. That means almost 2 out of every 5 websites you visit are powered by WordPress.

WordPress is an easy-to-use and powerful CMS that allows anyone to create a website without any coding experience. In this chapter, we will discuss the latest version of WordPress, version 6.x, and how you can get started with it.

WordPress 6.x: What's new

WordPress released version 6.2 on December 8th, 2020. As WordPress releases updates often, they are typically minor ones to fix bugs or security issues. However, there were some notable changes in the updated version:

- Automated WordPress Core updates

From here on, WordPress will be updated automatically to minor versions by default. Security and stability improvements are automatically applied to all sites.

- New blocks added to the block editor

Version 6.2 introduced some new blocks to the block editor, including a social icons block and a buttons block. These blocks make it easier to add social media icons or buttons to a page without having to resort to writing any code. More about that later.

- Bug fixes and enhancements

WordPress 6.2 also came with some bug fixes and enhancements, including improved block editor performance, better handling of navigation menus, and improved accessibility.

Now that you know what's new in WordPress 6, here's how to get started

- Choose a hosting provider and domain name:

Before you can install and use WordPress, you need a hosting provider and a domain name. In some cases, it comes down to the choice between being a small fish in a big pond or a fish in a small pond. The difference is often how long you have to wait for help or whether you find yourself communicating with a text robot or a voicemail. Think of a large company whose name starts with "G" or "M" and the last time you tried to reach somebody there.

If you are starting a new website, there are a great many hosting providers to choose from. Many will install and set up WordPress for you at no added cost. You can also host your WordPress website at WordPress.com. Keep in mind, the larger the company, the less easy it is to get personal attention to any problem that might arise.

Once you have chosen the hosting provider, you also need to choose a domain name (the website URL). You can also do that at Cyberchute.com. GoDaddy is the largest registrar, but there is one big disadvantage. If you are late renewing your domain name at GoDaddy or some of the other registrars, it's gone forever. Worse than that , it could be sold off to a foreign entity within hours. In some cases, a large "recovery" charge will be added. With other registrars, like ENOM/TuCows, there could be a "grace period" where you can recover and renew your domain registration.

Be wary of low cost domain registration. There is a certain "wholesale" cost for registering domain names. Any service that charges less than that cost, in most cases, will end up costing you more. For example, one registrar may charge $1.99 for the initial registration but will require a three-year registration. Every subsequent year will cost much above the average normal cost.

This brings up the point that you do not "own" your domain name, you only "rent" it by the year. That is just one of several reasons you may want to register your domain name for several years and maintain that margin of safety. Another is the fact that search engines award extra points for domains that are registered for more than one year. It demonstrates that you mean to stay around.

To answer another question that may arise, yes, more than one domain name can be assigned, or "aliased" to the same website. Ask your hosting provider tech support. There's even a way to have one domain name targeted to a specific page in another website. Smarter web hosts know how to do that. Smarter web hosts also know how to make the page automatically go to the secure HTTPS directory.

HTTPS or SSL Security is a must. That function adds security encryption. Why is that important? An HTTPS certificate assures the visitor that they are at the website they intended. SSL Certificates can be acquired at a cost ranging from free to a few dollars to a lot more.

Many hosting providers can install *LetsEncrypt* to provide basic security encryption for your website at no cost (free). Other SSL certificates provide higher levels of protection at a higher cost and are appropriate for shopping cart websites which store credit card information on the website. The cost reflects the level of encryption and/or the amount of insurance provided. However, if transactions are handled by a service, the actual transactions are not handled on the website where the purchase is being made and there is no reason for higher-level security. PayPal, Stripe, Authorize.Net and other transaction handlers have their own liability coverage.

The higher security certificates offer insurance options into the millions and can cost thousands per year. The average WordPress website needs only the basic (free) security certificate.

- Installing WordPress:

After you have chosen a hosting provider and domain name, you can install WordPress. Most hosting providers offer a one-click installation option for WordPress. If not, you can install WordPress manually by downloading the latest version from the WordPress website and following the installation instructions. You will need to have something called FTP access, which requires a username and password. These are not, however, options favored by beginners. You also have the option to host your website at WordPress.com.

- Choose a theme:

After you have installed WordPress, you need to choose a theme. A theme determines the overall look and feel of your website. WordPress has many free and paid themes to choose from. You can browse for themes in the WordPress theme directory or purchase themes from third-party websites like *ThemeForest*.

- Select and Install plugins:

A plugin is a piece of software that adds new functionality to WordPress. There are thousands of free and paid plugins available in the WordPress plugin directory. You can install plugins by going to the Plugins section in your WordPress dashboard and clicking on "Add New."

- Create your content:

Once your website is installed, you can start creating the content. In WordPress, there are two main content types: posts and pages. Posts are most often used for blog entries, while pages are used for static content like the "about" page or the "contact us" page. A page is a regular web page you are used to seeing. If a website offers a subscription, they are inviting you to receive emails when a new blog post is added. A blog post is something like a one-way version of social media, like Facebook or Twitter.

You can create posts and pages by going to those sections in your WordPress dashboard and selecting the "Add new."

Conclusion

WordPress 6.x is a powerful and easy-to-use content management system that allows anyone to create a website without any coding experience. It comes with many new features and enhancements to make the website-building process even easier. By following the steps in this chapter, you can get started with WordPress 6 and create your own website.

Chapter 3

The WordPress 6.x Dashboard

The WordPress 6.x Dashboard is the central control panel for managing your WordPress site. In this chapter, we will guide you through the various sections of the WordPress 6.x dashboard, including the Home Screen, Post, Pages, Media, Comments, Appearance, Plugins, Users, Tools, and Settings.

As a beginner in WordPress, the first thing that may seem overwhelming is the WordPress Dashboard. WordPress version 6.x has a user-friendly and intuitive dashboard that makes website management easy for beginners and advanced users alike. In this chapter, we will explore the WordPress 6.x dashboard in detail, its various components, and how to use them.

Introduction to the WordPress 6.x Dashboard

The WordPress 6.x dashboard is the main administrative page where website owners and editors can manage everything related to their website. Once you log in to your WordPress account, you will be redirected to the dashboard. The dashboard features numerous components that provide a complete overview of your website, including your latest posts, pages, comments, stats, and more.

Understanding the Menu Options

The WordPress 6.x dashboard is divided into several sections, with each section containing different menu options. The primary navigation menu is located on the left-hand side of the screen, while the submenus are positioned in the middle:

Some of the main menu options you will come across include:

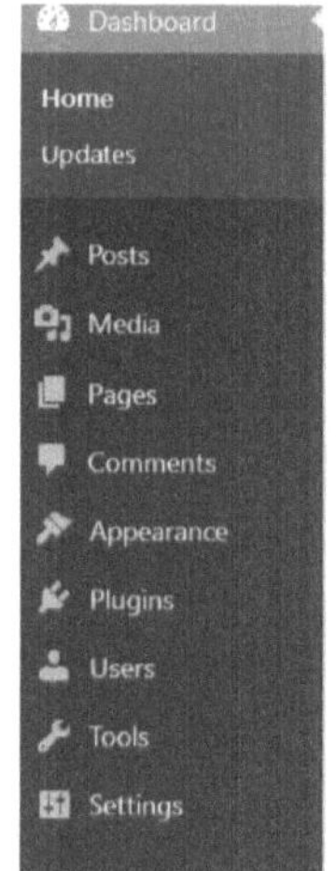

- Home: The home menu option takes you back to the main WordPress dashboard.

- Posts: This option allows you to create new posts, update existing ones, and manage your writing team.

- Media: The media menu is where you can upload, organize, and add media files to your website.

- Pages: The pages menu allows you to create and manage static pages, such as About Us, Contact Us, etc.

- Comments: The comments menu displays all the comments left on your website and lets you manage them. (Our recommendation is to disable comments.)

- Appearance: This menu option allows you to select and customize your website's theme, modify widgets, menus, and more.

- Plugins: The plugins menu allows you to install and manage your website's plugins.

- Users: This option allows you to manage your website's user accounts and set access levels.

- Tools: The tools menu is used to import and export data, scan for broken links, and more.

- Settings: This option includes setting options for General, Writing, Reading, Discussion (Comments), Media, Peramalinks and Privacy.

Understanding the Dashboard Widgets

Dashboard "Widgets" are like tiny pages that can be used in places like the left or right columns in a WordPress page, typically on the first page or alongside blog posts.

Apart from the menu options, the WordPress dashboard features various widgets that offer convenient access to important information about your website. The dashboard widgets are displayed on the right-hand side of the screen and can be customized to meet your specific needs. Widgets only appear in the administration screen and are not visible to the public viewing the website. There is another type of widget that is visible to the public which will be discussed later.

Some of the common dashboard widgets include:

- At a Glance: This widget provides a summary of your website's posts, pages, and comments.

- Quick Draft: The quick draft widget allows you to create new posts and save them as drafts directly from the dashboard.

- Activity: The activity widget displays important activity on your site, including recent comments, published posts, etc.

- WordPress News: This widget displays the latest news and updates from the WordPress community.

Dashboard widgets are not the same as the Widgets in the "Appearance" menu. Often there is a "search" box to the right side of the home page in a theme. You may see Widget displaying a list of blog posts. That's what a Widget is in Appearance. You'll find those and other options for various pages in the Widgets menu section.

Customizing Your Dashboard

The WordPress 6.x dashboard is highly customizable, and you can easily tailor it to meet your specific needs. You can rearrange the dashboard widgets, add or remove menu options, and more. You can also install plugins that add additional dashboard widgets that provide more information about your website's performance.

Conclusion

The WordPress 6.x dashboard is a central part of your website management. By understanding its various components, you can easily manage your website's content, monitor its performance, and make necessary adjustments to improve your website's user experience.

Chapter 4

Creating and Managing Posts

B log posts are the primary content on many websites. It can be argued that blog posts were the primary motive behind the creation and origin of WordPress. As the platform has evolved to include regular web pages and eCommerce and more. WordPress is not just for blogging any more.

In this chapter, we will guide you through the process of creating blog posts, or just "posts" in WordPress 6.x. We will show you how to use the post editor and add media, like pictures or videos, to categorize and tag your posts, and publish them using the WordPress template or "theme".

Creating and managing posts is an essential part of running a WordPress blog website. This chapter will guide you through the process of creating and managing posts in WordPress 6.x.

Creating a New Post

To create a new post, follow these steps:

1. Log in to your WordPress dashboard.

2. Click on the 'Posts' menu item on the left-hand side of the screen.

3. Click on the 'Add New' button at the top of the screen.

4. Enter the title of your post in the 'Add Title' field.

5. Write your post content in the 'Add Post' field using the Gutenberg editor.

6. Add tags and categories to your post. These help to organize your content and make it easier for your readers to find related posts.

7. Choose a featured image for your post. This will be displayed at the top of your post and on the homepage of your website, depending on the theme you are using.

8. Preview your post by clicking on the 'Preview' button.

When you are happy with your post, click on the 'Publish' button to make it live on your website.

Managing Posts

To manage your posts, follow these steps:

- Log in to your WordPress dashboard.

- Click on the 'Posts' menu item on the left-hand side of the screen.

Here, you will see a list of all the posts on your website. You can sort them by date, category, or tag.

To edit a post, hover over it and click on the 'Edit' button.

You can make changes to your post and then click the 'Update' button to save your changes. Otherwise, save as "draft" to come back to it later.

To delete a post, hover over it and click on the 'Trash' button that appears.

You can also use the 'Quick Edit' option to edit the title, slug (menu link), categories, and status of your posts without opening the full editor. (This is also where you can disable comments)

If you need to search for a specific post, use the search box at the top right of the screen.

The 'Categories' and 'Tags' menus allow you to add, edit, or delete post categories and tags.

Post Settings

WordPress allows you to customize various settings related to your posts. To access these settings, follow these steps:

Log in to your WordPress dashboard.

Click on the 'Settings' menu item on the left-hand side of the screen.

Go to the 'Writing' section.

Here, you can change the default post category, post format, and post editor.

You can also customize the default post status, comment settings, and pingbacks/trackbacks.

In the 'Media' section, you can customize how WordPress handles media files.

In the *'Permalinks'* section, you can customize the URL structure of your posts. In most cases, you will want to select *POST NAME*.

Conclusion

Blog posts don't always need to be used for blogs. For example, the post function can be an easy way to manage newsletters, for example. In combination with plugin functions like MailChimp or ConstantContact, the process of writing and delivering newsletters to a membership list can be automated, replacing the need for creating PDF files and attaching them to emails to members. It also relieves the manual function of adding and removing members from the members mailing list.

Search engines and directories like Google, Bing and Yahoo "love" fresh content, and news posts are a simple way of providing new things for your website visitors as well as keeping them informed.

Creating and managing posts in WordPress is easy and straightforward. With the steps outlined in this chapter, you can create great content and organize it in a way that makes it easy for your audience to find. Take time to explore the various post settings and see how they can be customized to fit your needs.

Chapter 5

Adding Media

M edia in WordPress can mean pictures, PDF files or videos.

At the top of the Media screen there are two options: Media Library and Add New.

As the screen indicates, you can either drag-and-drop files from your desktop or SE-LECT FILES from your computer. The default limit is 2 MB but your web host can adjust that limitation if necessary.

You don't really want to upload very large images, but you may need to raise the limit for large PDF files.

One nice benefit of the WordPress Media function is the built-in image editor. Click on an image stored in the library to open the editor. The editor provides for adding Alternative Text, an image title, caption and description. The Alternative Text provides a description for screen readers for the blind or disabled. The caption might be useful for including image source information or "CLICK" when a link is added to an image in a page or post. The edit screen also provides information about the file size and dimensions of the image, and other information.

Click on the EDIT button at the bottom of the displayed image to find a new menu:

Attachment details

Sometimes when you import a picture from your phone, it comes out sideways or upside down, and these controls will help you solve the problem by rotating left or right, or flipping vertically or horizontally. The remaining function is "CROP". Clicking on that function adds little box "handles" around the image. Adjust the boxes to select a smaller portion of the image. But don't stop there. You must remember to click the "Crop" button again to lock in your changes. The edit screen will automatically save your edits in a few seconds, so you can escape out of that screen to return to the Media function.

In most cases, it's probably best to avoid uploading videos directly to your website. There's a better way. Store video files off-server on YouTube or storage services like Vimeo. Those services are optimized for delivering videos and you won't fill up up your available hosting storage space.

Later we will show you how to use the Media function to add images and videos to a page or blog post on your website.

Chapter 6

Creating and Managing Pages

WordPress 6.x enables you to create and manage web pages using various tools. In this chapter, we will take you through the process of creating pages on WordPress 6.x using the WordPress Editor, *Elementor Page Builder*, and other options. We will also show you how to manage and organize the pages on your site. By the way, when we refer to 6.x we are referring to version 6 and the subsequent revisions after that.

Creating a New Page

Creating and managing pages is an essential part of building your WordPress website. In this section, we'll go over the basics of how to create, edit, and manage pages.

To create a new page in WordPress, start by logging into your WordPress dashboard and going to the "Pages" section. Click on the "Add New" button at the top of the screen.

Content Blocks

In the original WordPress and even in HTML it was difficult to arrange text and images in the desired places on a page. Blocks are designed to make it simpler for users to create and customize their website's content layout. Initially referred to as *Gutenberg Blocks*, the WordPress "Blocks" feature was introduced in version 5.

When you enter a page with Blocks enabled, you are provided with a series of orientation pop-ups. It's a good idea to go through the series to become familiar with the function. Once you dismiss the pop-up you will not be bothered by it in the future.

First, it is important to understand what Blocks are. Blocks refers to the *building blocks* of WordPress content. They are constructed from individual elements like paragraphs, images, headings, lists, files, videos, buttons, etc. that can be added to posts and pages. Previously, users had to use custom code or plugins to achieve similar results.

Using Blocks in WordPress is very easy. Here are the steps:

Step 1: Create a new post or page in WordPress.

Step 2: Click on the "+" button, in the top left corner of the editing space:

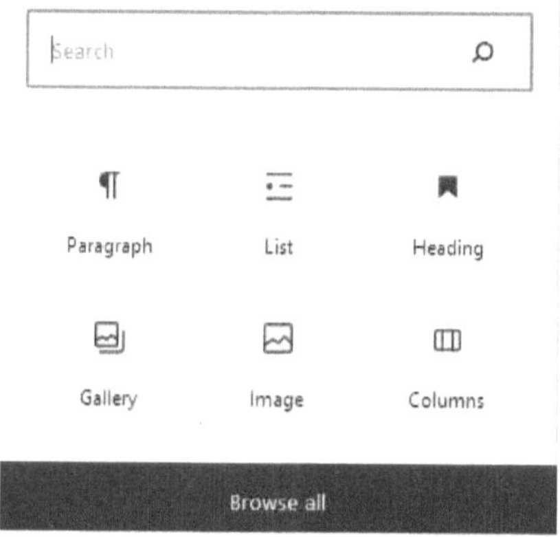

Step 3: A list of available Block functions will appear. The default is text or paragraph. You can select from the most common functions or use the search box. Select Columns to split the block into two2 or more sections. Select functions like a photo gallery, heading, bullet list, YouTube or Vimeo videos, contact forms or images. For example, select *Columns* and place an image in the left block and text in the right. Or the other way around, if it suits your purpose. You could then select a single column for subsequent text on the page. Selecting IMAGE will take you to the Media Library where you can import or select a media file. The "Select" function will appear in the lower right side of the media screen.

Step 4: Once you have found the Block function you want, click on it, and it will be added to your post or page.

Step 5: You can customize the Block by editing its settings, like changing the text size, color, or font.

Step 6: Once you have added two or more Blocks to a page, you can move the Blocks up or down by clicking the "move" functions on the pop-up insert.

Step 7: If you want to add more Blocks, just repeat the process by selecting the "+" when you mouse over an open section of a page.

Step 8: Once you have completed the editing of your post or page, click to "UPDATE" it. Remember you will find the blue UPDATE button in the upper right corner of the main editing screen.

Blocks are also very customizable. With advanced training you can add custom CSS (Cascading Style Sheets formatting) classes, write your own HTML, and even use blocks to build mini-layouts within larger posts. You can also save Blocks that you use frequently as reusable templates.

If you have Blocks disabled with a plugin such as "Classic Editor"

Adding a new page will take you to the basic page editor, where you can begin building your new page. Your page editor should look something like this:

Here, you can add a title for your new page, as well as any content you want to include. You can also use the formatting tools provided to format your text, add images, and more.

Notice below Add title where it says "Add media". Place your cursor on the page where you need to add an image or media file and then click the Add Media button. That will take you to the Media screen where you can import or choose an image file. At the lower right on that screen you will find a "Select" button which will bring you back to your page or post to place the media file.

Extra line of editing options will appear when you click the "toolbar toggle" which is the icon that looks like three bars with dots or SHIFT + ALT + Z

Once you've finished creating your new page, click the "Publish" button to make it live on your website. You'll find it near the top right corner of the WordPress screen.

Editing an Existing Page

To edit an existing page, simply go to the "Pages" section of your WordPress dashboard and find the page you want to edit. Mouse over the page title. A submenu will appear. Click on the EDIT to open the page editor.

From here, you can edit or change any of the text or content on the page, add new content, or delete existing content. Once you've finished editing the page, click the "Update" button to save your changes. If your website was created in the Classic mode, you can select "Convert to blocks". From there you can add columns and place any images where they should fit on the page.

What about adding video?

Adding video to a website makes it stand out from a static website. The downside is that videos are very large files. Another downside, is that hosting servers are not really optimized for displaying video. There's a better answer. Let somebody else do the work.

As we mentioned earlier , the most obvious solution is YouTube. YouTube hosts the your gigantic video file for free and provides a two ways to place it on your website.

In the + menu, search "video":

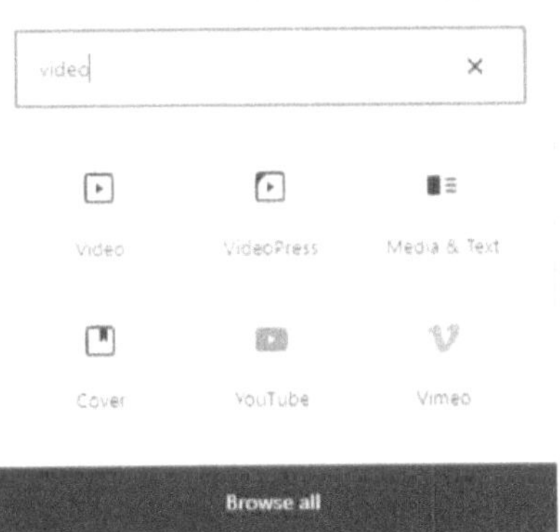

You will notice you have several source choices. The first choice is labeled simply "video" and it looks like this:

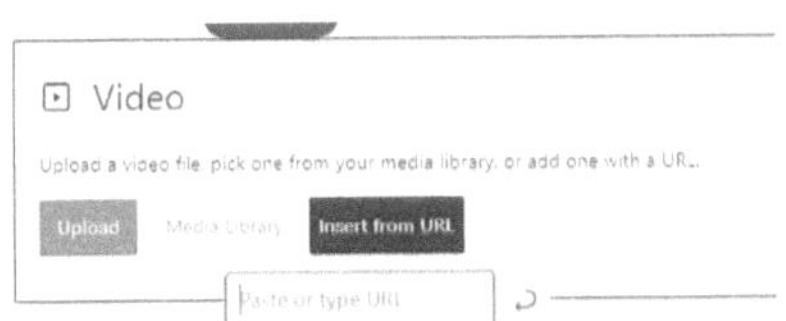

We mentioned before it's probably best not to upload large video files because they may be slow. Type or paste the video link into the Insert from URl box and enter or click the curved arrow.

The most obvious choices are YouTube and Vimeo. For YouTube, click the "Share" function under the video display and you will see this:

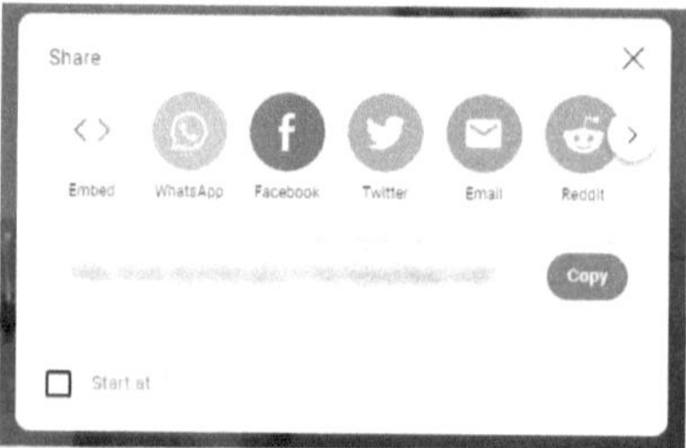

Use the COPY function to capture the link and then paste it (Ctrl+V for Windows) into the box marked "Enter URL to embed here…" as shown.

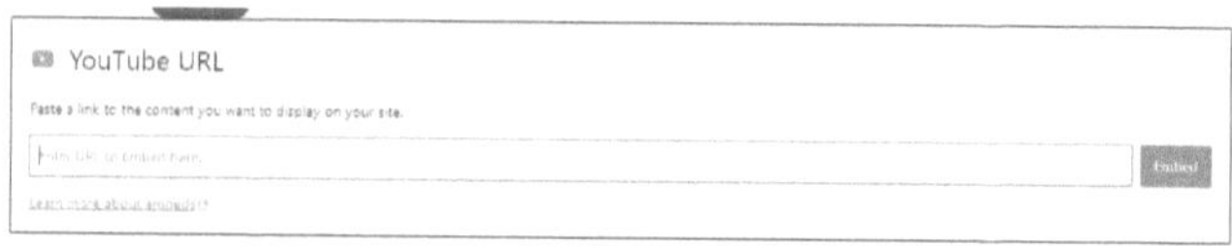

The same process applies to videos hosted on Vimeo.

There is yet another way to "embed" a YouTube or Vimeo video.

For this you would need to copy the EMBED code and paste it into the box and click "Embed".

PDF Files

Sometimes you want to include PDF files for download on your website. Adding a "file" is as easy as adding an image from your Media directory. select the FILE selection:

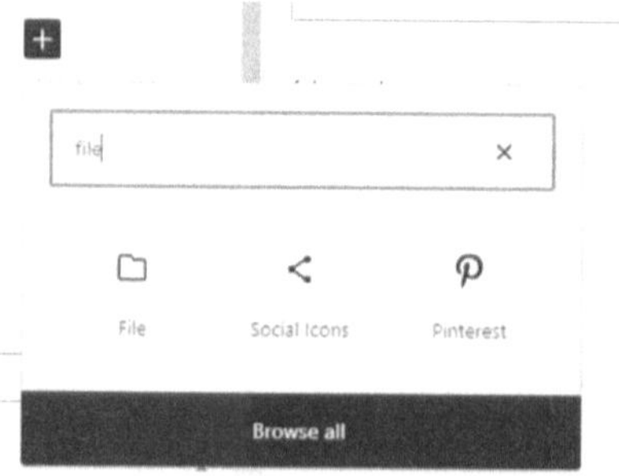

Once you have selected or uploaded your PDF file you have several options:

Show Inline Embed will display an active image of the PDF file. If you deselect this function the file will show as a download without the preview image, assuming you have left the default "Show download button" on.

Another option is to "Open in new tab". For visitors viewing your website on a phone or tablet, it's probably best to leave that function turned off (disabled).

Advanced: Anchor link

You may have noticed on a website that a link takes you not to the top of a page, but to a section in that page. That function is accomplished with what is known as an "anchor" tag. For example, if you have a Subscription section in your Contact page, you can send visitors directly to that part of the Contact page.

Here's how it works:

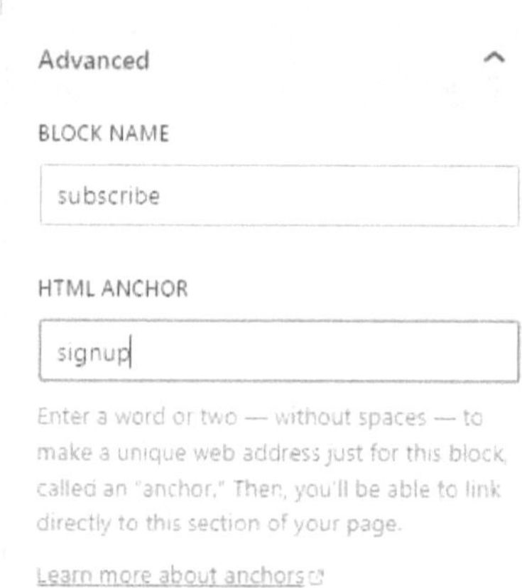

The link "Learn more about anchors" explains how it works in detail, but in practice you would link to that section like this:

website.com/contact#signup

When the page is complete, look for the blue update button in the top right corner of the screen:

Managing Pages

As you continue to add and edit pages on your WordPress website, you'll want to keep track of them all to ensure that they're all working correctly and providing value to your visitors.

To manage your pages, start by going to the "Pages" section of your WordPress dashboard. Here, you'll see a list of all your existing pages, along with information about each one, such as its title, author, and status (published, draft, or pending review).

From this screen, you can perform a variety of actions, such as deleting pages, editing pages, and previewing pages (to see how they'll look to visitors).

If you have a large number of pages, you can use the *search* and *filter* options at the top-right part of the screen to find specific pages or organize your pages by criteria such as date published, author, or status.

By staying on top of your pages and keeping them organized and up-to-date, you'll create a better user experience for your visitors and help your website grow and succeed.

Visual/Text

If you happen to be "old school" enough to remember HTML, you may find the Text view function useful. Hiding inside your WordPress page is familiar HTML. If you have that skill, there could be rare instances where it could come in handy. For example, if an <h2> headline code insists on affecting the next three lines, you can move the </h2> back to where it belongs.

For the beginner, however, it's best to "look but do not touch" in the Text function. To return to the normal Visual editing mode, just click the Visual tab.

Chapter 7

Comments

O nce upon a time, comments provided a means for useful engagement of website visitors. Unfortunately, the Comments function has become a common target for abuse. If you leave comments enabled, you will quickly find your website overrun with spam messages hawking drugs and worse. For that reason, it is best to disable Comments for blog posts and pages.

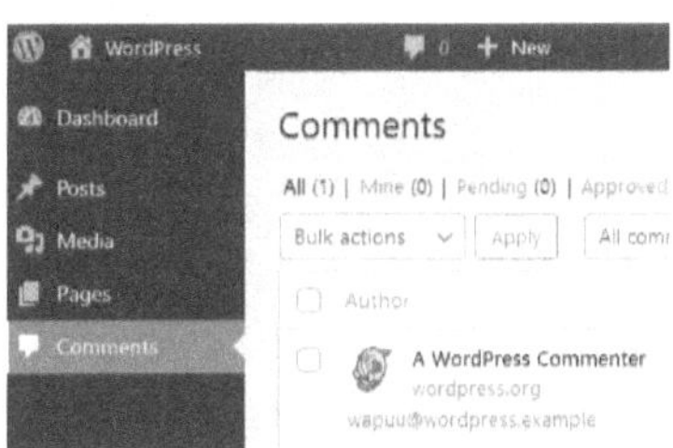

Here's how to block comments from flooding your website:

In Posts/All Posts, move your mouse over each post and select "Quick Edit".

On the Quick Edit screen, ***uncheck*** the box for Allow Comments.

Next, go to Settings, Discussion and uncheck all the comment boxes.

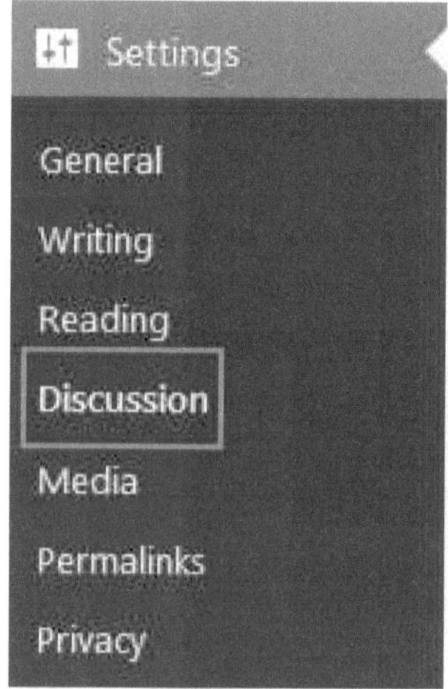

If you forget to block comments and discover hundreds or thousands posted on your site, you don't need to remove them one by one. There's a plugin for that.

Go to Plugins, then either in the drop-down menu or at the top of the page select "Add New". IN the search box on the right side of the screen type in "Remove Comments" Select a suitable comment remover tool that is Compatible with your version of WordPress and has an adequate number of 5-star ratings. Be careful! Try to avoid any plugins with no installations, no ratings or are "Untested with your version of WordPress". One good choice might be *Disable Comments* by WPDeveloper with 1+ million installations.

Chapter 8

Appearance

Under the Appearance section in the Dashboard, there are most often several sections. The first function is Themes, which we will cover in the next chapter. Below that is Editor. This function should be reserved for advanced users only. Best to look, but don't touch. Click the Back arrow or the WordPress logo to escape from this page.

- **Themes** (This item is covered in the following chapter) The first theme on the left is the one that is currently "active".

- **Customize** This is one of several ways to reach the customizing functions, for managing the page header, the content of the front (home) page (static or blog), footer content and other features unique to the currently active theme. This item is covered in more detail in the following chapter.

- **Widgets** These are items which may appear to the right of page content. An example would be the Search box or a list of blog posts. There can be a widget to list blog categories. Widgets many be used for adding content to a website's footer section. Widgets can be added, arranged or removed. Typically, widgets appear in the right column on the main page of a website and alongside blog posts.

- **Menus** This can be the main menu at the top of the page or a menu that appears in the bottom of "footer' of the website. This section manages which pages are linked to menu tabs on the website. Note, common practice is to place the Contact tab on the right end of the main menu. Select which pages will appear in the menu and choose "add". That item will appear at the bottom of the list.

Click and drag the menu item where you want it to appear. Clicking and moving a menu to the right forms a kind of stair step for a submenu or "drop-down" tab.

- **Background** Here is where you can select an appropriate background image or color for your website. Avoid using "busy" images with a lot of detail that will conflict with the text content of your website. Many themes come with backgrounds already set. However, an off white background can minimize the glaring contrast between black text and a white background. In other cases, the same effect can be achieved by softening the font color.

- **Theme File Editor** This screen comes with a *Heads up!* warning. If you purchased this book because of "Beginner" in the title, it would be best to heed the warning and click the button to "Go back". *Hint: I've been this for decades and I don't go there unless I really need to.*

There may be a subsection under Appearance to *Import Demo Content.* You may wish to do that for a new website or Theme, but if you import content to an existing website, you may find your nicely composed text content and images have been replaced by "samples" and examples.

Most often the images you see in the theme preview are NOT included and are examples of what the theme could look like.

By the way, the sample or "filler" text content you will most likely encounter at some point, which reads like Latin, is not an actual language. It's known as *Lorem Ipsum*, which are the words most likely to appear in the first line of text.

Here's the history. With the rise of printing and typesetting in the 16th century, printers, and typesetters used the seemingly random groups of letters as a placeholder to show various fonts and designs without the distraction of actual content. Over time, it became the standard dummy text in the printing industry, which found its way to a similar use in digital "typesetting" for desktop publishing, word processors, design programs and websites.

The phrase *"Lorem ipsum dolor sit amet"* can be traced to the works of the Roman philosopher and statesman Cicero. However, the *Lorem Ipsum* text as we know it today is not directly derived from Cicero's writings. Maybe that could come up in a trivia game, or maybe not.

Chapter 9

WordPress Themes

Appearance

Themes are pre-designed templates that give your WordPress site a unique look and feel. In this chapter, we will guide you through the process of selecting and installing themes on your WordPress site. We will also discuss customizing the theme to fit your branding and content.

WordPress 6.x comes with default theme installed along with a variety of other themes to choose from. A theme is like a skin for your website. It determines the overall look and layout of your site. You can choose a theme that suits your needs, or you can customize one to your liking.

Here's how you can use themes in WordPress 6.x:

1. Log in to your WordPress site.

2. Go to Appearance > Themes.

3. You'll see examples of available free themes. Use the "filter" to narrow your choices. Ignore the sample graphics and images you see in the samples. Those are most often not included. Mouse-over any you would like to preview to reveal "Theme Details", or to "Activate" or you can choose to view "Live Preview". The preview will display your current content without affecting the current site unless you select "Activate".

4. When you find a theme you like, click on the "Activate" button to apply it to your site. If you activate a new theme, you may need to make adjustments to adapt your content to the new design. If you decide you liked the other theme

better you can always go back and Activate that one or search for another one.

You are not limited to the thousands of free theme designs. There are many more paid theme sources, including ThemForest.net (Envato), TemplateMonster, ElegantThemes, StudioPress, Themify, and the list goes on. Some of the free themes also offer upgrades, often to include support services. Search "WordPress themes" online for more options.

Customizing Your Theme

Most themes come with some customizations that you can make to suit your specific needs.

When we say "Go to" in this context, most often we are referring to one of the selections in the left side Dashboard. Here's how you can customize your WordPress 6.x theme:

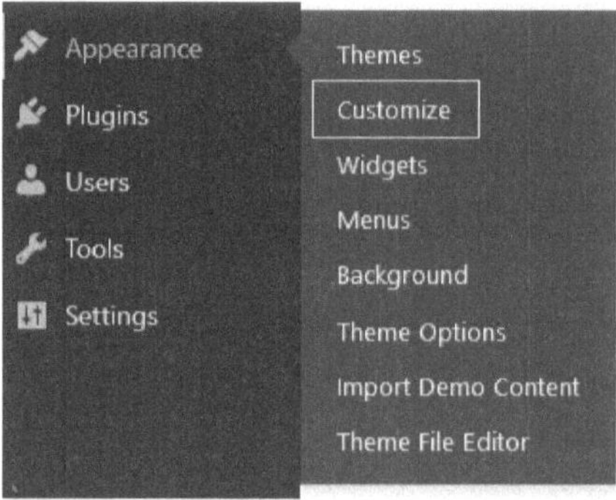

1. Go to Appearance -> Customize.

2. You'll then see a list of options that you can customize. For example, you can change the header image, the widget settings, and the background color.

3. *Each theme has a different set of customizing features.* With each option you customize, you'll see a preview of how it will look on your site.

4. Once you're satisfied with your customizations and changes, click "Save & Publish" to apply the changes to your site. If you forget and try to leave the page without saving, WordPress will warn that your changes won't be stored.

A theme does not need to match your exact purpose or use. The theme is really just the layout arrangement. For example, you may find that a theme designed for a florist will work just fine for a veterinarian practice or a photographer's portfolio.

One note of caution: If your web developer makes major modifications to a theme, those changes may not be compatible with future theme updates by the original developer.

Automatic Theme Feeds

Don't be surprised to see new themes appearing in the Themes section. WordPress sometimes adds new themes along with other updates. At least once a year, WordPress releases a new "default" theme. However, those extra themes take up file space, and best practice is to remove any you don't need, especially if your site is on a scheduled backup. However, you will want to keep one spare theme in reserve in case your current theme becomes outdated or abandoned by the developer. If you don't plan to use the new themes, it's a good idea to remove (delete) them. Mouse over the unwanted theme, click the Theme Details option, then click the red "delete" at the bottom of the pop-in screen.

In that same section, you will want to keep your active theme up to date when a new update is available. That's another reason to visit your site's admin screen at least once a week, even if you don't have anything new to add.

Conclusion

Using themes and plugins in WordPress 6.x can help you create a dynamic and engaging website. Don't be afraid to experiment with different themes and plugins until you find the ones that work best for your site. Remember, the key is to create a site that looks great, is easy to navigate, and is full of useful content for your readers, but most of all, the theme must suit your needs and purpose.

Chapter 10

WordPress Plugins

P lugins are additional features that add functionality to your WordPress site. In this chapter, we will introduce you to some of the essential plugins you need to have on your site, how to search and install plugins, and how to manage them in the WordPress administrator site.

In this chapter, we will discuss the importance of plugins in WordPress and introduce some popular plugins that can help enhance your website's functionality.

Understanding Plugins

Plugins are software components that can be added to a WordPress website to add specific features and functionalities to the site. They allow users to add new features to their websites without the need for extensive coding or development work. With a plugin, you can add new functionalities to your website, such as security features, contact forms, social media integration, and more.

CAUTION – Some plugins will include a warning "Untested with your version of WordPress". Also note the number of Active Installations and when the plugin was last updated. Click on More Details to check the Reviews. Avoid using untested plugins with few installations and poor reviews. When you find a plugin you think you would like, check the Installation to see how to implement your selection. If a plugin developer abandons a plugin, it is recommended you find an active plugin to provide the same function and delete and uninstall outdated themes.

Popular WordPress Plugins

WordPress offers a wide range of plugins that can be used for free or purchased at a reasonable cost. Here are some of the most popular WordPress plugins:

- **WPForms**
  WPForms is a user-friendly drag-and-drop form builder plugin that allows users to create customizable contact forms, surveys, polls, and more. It also includes several pre-built templates that make it easy to create professional-looking forms.

- **Contact Form 7**
  Contact Form 7 is a free plugin that lets users create customizable contact forms on their website. It features a user-friendly drag-and-drop interface, customizable forms, and spam protection features. An email address can be linked from a web page by adding "mailto:" in front of the link to the email address. However, it is best to use a contact form to prevent spammers from "harvesting" exposed email addresses from your website.

- **reCaptcha:** Spammers can also attack a contact form, which is why you may want to add re Captcha integration. re Captcha is a free utility from Google. You may need some technical assistance. You may want to search for reCaptcha or look for videos on YouTube for help.

- **Jetpack**
  Jetpack is a powerful WordPress plugin that offers a suite of features, including website security, backups, and performance optimization. It also includes several tools for social media integration, website stats, and image optimization.

- **SEO**
  See the section on ***Optimization of WordPress for Search Engines*** for a sample of plugins available for that purpose.

- **WooCommerce**
  WooCommerce is a powerful plugin for building an online store (shopping cart) with WordPress. It provides the tools to customizable product pages, manage

inventory and shipping, and process payments securely.

- **WordFence**

  WordFence is a security monitoring plugin that can protect your website. The basic plugin is free and there are optional upgrades. No WordPress installation should be without WordFence. More on that in a later chapter on WordPress Security.

- **AI Tools**

  The most recent additions to the plugin toolbox are tools powered by Artificial Intelligence, such as 10Web AI Assistant, AI Engine, AI powered Search Engine Optimization tools, and even an Ai ChatBot plugin.

- **Other Plugins**

  There are literally thousands of plugins. WordPress plugins offer an excellent way to add new features and functionalities to your website quickly and easily. For example, and Events plugin can provide management for the display of scheduled programs and events, placing the next event at the top of the page.

We will explore plugins that provide enhanced editing and display features in the **section Where do you go from here? in the Conclusion chapter of this book.**

There are many plugins which provide both free and advanced (paid) options. For the plugin developer, the free versions serve as a means of marketing for the paid versions. With the right plugins, you can optimize your website for search engines, create custom contact forms, improve your website's performance, add extra features beyond what is available in the basic WordPress, and more.

Explore the many plugins available for WordPress but only choose those which best suit your website's needs. You will want to set the plugins to "Automatic Update" when available. Be careful, however, not to add too many plugins. For example, you may want to avoid plugins that generate pop-up screens which may annoy visitors. Always *Disable* and *Uninstall* plugins you are no longer using.

The reasons will be discussed in the chapter ***"What Could Go Wrong?"***

Chapter 11

Managing WordPress Users

Wordpress 6.x allows the administrator to add users to the site and give them different levels of permissions.

In WordPress 6.x, managing user roles can be accomplished in several ways. User roles can be edited or deleted, and new roles can be created to fit specific needs or functions.

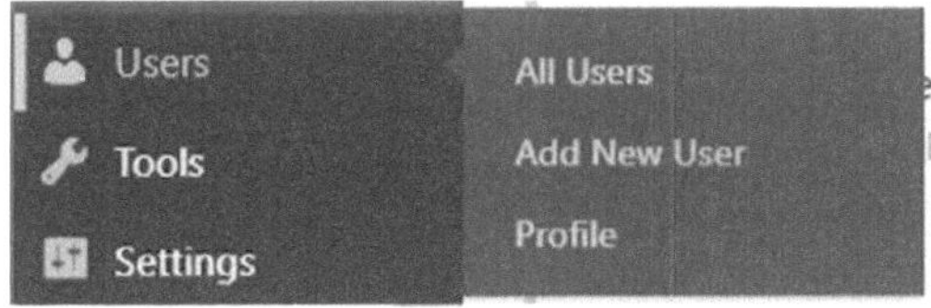

Understanding User Roles

First, it is essential to understand the different user roles in WordPress. By default, Word-Press provides six user roles:

1. Administrator: This is the most powerful user role in WordPress. Administrators can create, edit and delete pages, posts, user accounts, and other content.

2. Editor: Allows a user to manage and publish posts and pages, as well as moderate comments.

3. Author: Allows a user to create and publish their own posts.

4. Contributor: This user can write and submit posts, but cannot publish them. Editors or Administrators must approve and publish the posts.

5. Subscriber: This level of user can only view but cannot create or modify content.

6. Super Admin: This level is only available if WordPress Multisite is enabled. The Super Admin role has access to all the associated WordPress sites on the network.

Managing User Roles

The next step is to manage the users. There are several ways to do that in WordPress.

Built-In User Roles Editor:

One option to manage user roles is through the built-in User Roles Editor in WordPress. To use this method:

1. Log in to your WordPress dashboard

2. Navigate to Users > Edit User

3. Click on the Role dropdown

4. Select a new role for the user and click Save

Using this method, you can quickly change the role of an individual user. However, this method is not ideal for managing multiple users' roles, because it requires editing each user individually. You can't delete the user identity that you are logged in as. Only administrators can modify other users. For that reason, be careful who you grant administrator access to.

Use a Plugin

Another way to manage user roles is by using a plugin. Some of the most popular plugins for managing user roles include:

1. User Role Editor: This plugin lets you manage user roles, capabilities, and permissions with ease. You can add new roles, delete roles, and change the permissions for each role.

2. Members: A user role and plugin management plugin that enables you to specify which users have access to specific content on your site.

3. Advanced Access Manager: This plugin gives you the ability to control and restrict user access for your WordPress website. It includes features such as the ability to define custom user roles, assign roles to custom post types, and restrict user access to specific pages and posts.

4. Create Custom User Roles

Custom User role

The last way to manage user roles is to ***create a custom user role***. This method is useful if none of the built-in user roles fit your website's specific needs. Here's how to create a custom user role:

1. Install and activate the Members plugin.

2. Navigate to Users > Roles > Add New

3. Enter a name for the custom role and click on the Add Role button

4. From the Role Capabilities section, assign specific capabilities to the new role

Creating custom user roles provides more control over the website's content and modifications. The administrator can grant or restrict access to various features and actions, ensuring that only allowed users have control over content.

User roles play a critical role in managing a WordPress website. By understanding the options available and implementing the right methods, the administrator (owner or developer) can manage user roles effectively. That can be accomplished by using the built-in User Role Editor, employing a plugin, or creating custom user roles to achieve the best results.

One important security caution is to **NEVER share your administrator login and password.** Anyone you give administrator level access to can REMOVE you r access and take over your website. Don't provide a higher level of access to a user who does not need it to perform their assigned tasks.

Chapter 12

Settings

In the Settings menu, you will find:

- **General:** On this screen you can add your site title, a tagline, the WordPress Address (URL) which most often links to your title or logo to provide for a quick way to return to the Home Page. This is where you can add your administrator contact email, time zone and preferred date and time display format along with which day your week starts with. This last item is most often only important if your website includes an events calendar of some type..

- **Writing:** This section will allow you to set your preferred Default Editor for all users. The options are Classic Editor and Block Editor. You can also select whether assigned users can choose between editors.

- **Reading:** This section duplicates what usually appears in the Appearance: Customize screen. Here you can choose whether the Homepage of your website contains either blog posts or a normal static page. If you have a separate blog page, you can assign which blank page will be used for that purpose. When posts are published, the will appear on this page in reverse order. The most recent post will appear first.

- **Discussion:** We covered this section earlier in the section on *Comments*. It's probably best to uncheck all the Comments boxes.

- **Media:** Most likely you can leave this page with the default settings.

- **Permalinks:** This is how your pages will appear in the browser address bar.

You'll most likely want to select Post Name.

- **Privacy:** This section provides the ability to generate a new Privacy Policy page for your website. Click the CREATE button and follow the directions by modifying the suggested text to suit your needs and requirements. Most often, the *Privacy* page appears in the footer section of a website, possibly along with a *Terms of Service* page.

There may be other settings listed for specific plugin functions.

Chapter 13

Optimization for Search Engines

Have you ever wondered why some websites appear higher (rank better) in search results than others? It's because of SEO or Search Engine Optimization, the process of optimizing your website to rank higher in search engine results pages.

WordPress is one of the most popular content management systems (CMS) out there. And while WordPress is great for creating and publishing content, it doesn't automatically optimize your site for search engines. That's why SEO is crucial if you want to attract more organic traffic to your WordPress site.

In this chapter, we'll introduce you to the world of WordPress SEO. We'll cover the basics, including what SEO is, why it's important, and how it works. Additionally, we will provide you with an overview of the factors that influence search engine rankings, such as keyword research, content optimization, and backlinks.

Search engine optimization (SEO) is crucial for any website to rank higher on search engine results pages (SERPs). In this chapter, we will guide you through the optimization of your WordPress 6.x site for SEO, including keyword research, content optimization, and technical SEO.

In this section, we'll discuss the different ways you can optimize your WordPress 6.x website for search engine optimization (SEO). SEO plays a crucial role in ensuring your website's visibility, ranking, and overall success. Here are some tips and techniques you can follow to optimize your site for SEO:

What is Search Engine Optimization (SEO)?

SEO is a set of techniques used to optimize your website to rank higher in search engine results pages (SERPs). The goal of SEO is to attract more organic traffic to your site, which in turn, can help you generate more leads, sales, or conversions.

Search engines like Google and Bing use complex algorithms to determine which websites appear at the top of search results for a particular query (see "keywords"). SEO is about understanding these algorithms and optimizing your website accordingly.

The ultimate goal of SEO is to increase the public *visibility* of your website and to attract or drive more traffic. To optimize your website for search engines, you need to consider things such as keyword research, on-page optimization, link building, and content creation.

- **Keyword Research:** Start by identifying the specific keywords and phrases that your target audience is using to search for content related to your niche. There are many online tools available that can help you with this.

- **On-Page Optimization:** Optimize your website's title tags, meta descriptions, headers, and content based on the keywords you have chosen. This improves the relevance of your website for those keywords.

- **Link Building:** Acquire high-quality backlinks from reputable websites to your web pages. This improves the authority and credibility of your website in the eyes of search engines.

- **Content Creation:** Create high-quality, engaging content that provides value to your target audience. This improves the relevance and authority of your website and also encourages link building.

Understanding how search engines work is crucial when it comes to optimizing your website for better ranking. SEO is an ongoing process, and it requires continuous efforts to keep up with the ever-changing search engine algorithms. However, if done correctly, it can bring significant benefits to your website's traffic and growth.

Why is SEO Important for Your WordPress Site

SEO is important because it can help you attract more organic traffic to your WordPress site. Organic traffic refers to users who find your site by typing in relevant keywords or phrases into a search engine.

The higher your site ranks in search engine results pages, the more likely it is to be clicked on by users. According to a study by Chitika, the top result on Google's first page gets 33% of the traffic, while the second result gets 18%, and the third result gets 11%.

In addition, SEO can help you improve the user experience on your site. When you optimize your content for search engines, you're also making it more accessible and valuable to your audience. This can lead to longer time on site, increased engagement, and higher conversions.

How Does SEO Work?

By following these tips and techniques, you can optimize your WordPress website for SEO and improve your website's visibility, ranking, and overall success.

As a WordPress site owner, it's important to invest time and effort into optimizing your site for search engines if you want to attract more organic traffic and grow your business. In the next chapter, we'll dive deeper into keyword research, one of the most important aspects of SEO.

- Understanding Search Engines

- How search engines work

- Common search engine algorithms

- Types of search engine results pages (SERPs)

Importance of search engine optimization for WordPress websites

In this section, we will take a closer look at search engines and how they work. Search engines are the backbone of the internet and without them, it would be impossible to find anything on the web. In order to optimize your website for search engines, you need to understand how they operate.

What is a Search Engine?

A search engine is a software tool that enables users to search the internet for content based on specific keywords or phrases. The search engine crawls through the web, indexes the content, and makes it available to users who are searching for it.

Search engines have become an integral part of our daily lives and are used billions of times every day. Some of the most popular search engines include Google, Bing, and Yahoo.

How Search Engines Work

Search engines operate through a complex algorithm that crawls the web and indexes content. The algorithm uses a set of rules to determine the relevance and quality of content and then ranks it accordingly. The ranking of content is determined by the search engine's search criteria. That search criteria typically includes things such as relevance, quality, and authority.

Search engines use a three-stage process for indexing content:

1. Crawling: Search engines crawl the web and find content to index

2. Indexing: Search engines then index the content they have found and store it in their database

3. Ranking: Search engines then rank the indexed content based on their search criteria and display it in the search engine results pages (SERPs)

Use SEO-friendly themes and plugins:

Choose themes and plugins that are SEO-friendly and optimized for search engines. This helps ensure that your website follows the best practices for SEO and is properly optimized for search engines. Make sure to pay attention to factors like page speed, mobile responsiveness, and schema markup.

For example, Yoast SEO is an all-in-one SEO plugin that helps optimize your website for search engines. It provides users with suggestions on how to improve their website's search engine rankings, such as adding meta descriptions and titles, optimizing images, and more.

Optimize your site structure:

Properly structuring your WordPress website can help search engines easily crawl and index your content. Use categories and tags correctly, create an XML sitemap, and optimize your URL structure.

Optimize your content:

Ensure that your content is optimized for keywords and phrases that are relevant to your audience and that you include high-quality, engaging, and unique content. Use internal linking and optimize your images with alt tags and proper file names.

Use meta descriptions and title tags:

Meta descriptions and title tags are snippets of text that appear in search engine result pages (SERPs). They provide users with a brief overview of your page's content and can significantly impact user click-through rates. Ensure that your meta descriptions and title tags are optimized for search engines.

Use responsive design:

Ensure that your website is optimized for all devices and screen sizes. Using a responsive design can improve user experience, thereby improving your website's bounce rates and overall rankings.

Use social media:

Social media is a powerful tool that can help you promote your website's content and build your online reputation. Utilize social media platforms to share your WordPress content and connect with your audience.

Monitor and improve your site's performance:

By using analytical tools and monitoring your website's performance, you can identify opportunities to improve your site's SEO and overall performance. Use tools like Google Analytics and Search Console to track your website's progress.

On-Page Optimization

On-page SEO refers to optimizing the content on your website's pages. This includes things like:

- Keyword research and selection: Understanding what keywords your users are searching for and incorporating them into your content.

- Title tags and meta descriptions: Writing compelling title tags and meta descriptions that accurately represent the content on your pages. These elements appear in search engine results pages and can impact click-through rates.

- Header tags: (H1, H2, H3) to structure your content and make it easier for users to read.

- Content optimization (including keyword placement, length, and density)

- Image optimization: Optimizing your images by compressing them, using descriptive file names, and adding alt tags that describe the image's content.

- Content Optimization: Creating high-quality, valuable content that includes relevant keywords and provides answers to users' questions.

- URL structure

- Internal linking

- Outbound links

On-Page Optimization is a powerful strategy used to improve the visibility and ranking of a website within search engine results pages (SERPs). The goal of on-page optimization is to make sure that your website content is both relevant and easily accessible to both users and search engine crawlers alike.

There are many factors that can affect your on-page optimization. Some of these factors include page titles, meta descriptions, headers, images, content, keyword placement, and internal linking structures, among others. In order to optimize your website's on-page performance, it is important to understand these factors and how they work together to improve your website's ranking in search results.

One of the most important aspects of on-page optimization is creating quality content that is relevant to your target audience. Your website should include content that is informative, engaging, and useful to potential visitors. Additionally, your content should include relevant keywords that can help search engines decipher what your website is all about. This will improve the chances of your website appearing in search results for keywords related to your business or industry.

Another important element of on-page optimization is proper use of titles and meta descriptions. These elements provide a brief summary of what each page on your website is all about. By optimizing these elements, you can help search engines understand what each page on your site is about, which can help you rank higher in search results.

Additionally, headers and subheads can help break up your content into manageable sections. This makes it easier for users to read and scan your content, which makes it more likely that they will stay on your website and engage with your content.

Images and videos are other important elements on your website that should be optimized for on-page performance. Proper use of alt-text and descriptive file names can help search engines understand what each image or video is about. Additionally, optimized file sizes and formats can help speed up your website's load time, which can improve both your user experience and search engine rankings.

Overall, on-page optimization is an essential component of any SEO strategy. By optimizing your website's content, titles, descriptions, headers, images, videos, and other elements, you can improve your website's visibility, user experience, and search engine ranking.

Off-Page Optimization

Off-page SEO refers to optimizing the factors outside of your website that impact your search engine rankings. This includes things like:

- Backlinking strategies: Getting other websites to link to your site. The more authoritative the site linking to you, the better.

- Importance of social media sharing and optimization: Building a social media presence and sharing your content on social media platforms.

- Directory listings and citations: Optimizing your site for local search by using local keywords and building local citations.

- Guest blogging and outreach

- Building an online community and reputation management: encouraging customers to leave reviews of your business on third-party review sites like Yelp or Google My Business.

Off-page optimization is an essential aspect of search engine optimization (SEO). It is a process of improving a website's visibility through external factors or signals that are beyond the website's control. This includes building high-quality backlinks, social media marketing, guest blogging, influencer outreach, and other promotional activities.

The primary objective of off-page optimization is to enhance a site's credibility and reputation in the eyes of search engines, resulting in higher rankings and increased visibility on search engine result pages (SERPs). Off-page optimization is critical because search engines view links from external sources as a vote of confidence in a website's content. Therefore, the more high-quality backlinks a site has from authoritative websites, the higher its ranking in search engines.

Another key factor of off-page optimization is social media marketing. Social media platforms provide a vast opportunity to reach a large audience and promote a website's content. Through social media marketing, a website can build a loyal following, create engagement, and generate more traffic, which can indirectly enhance its search engine rankings.

Guest blogging is another effective off-page optimization technique. Guest blogging involves writing valuable and informative content for websites within the same niche or industry. By doing so, the website can build relationships with other websites, increase backlinks, and reach a new audience that can potentially visit and share the content.

Influencer outreach is also a powerful off-page optimization strategy. Influencer marketing involves collaborating with individuals or brands that command a significant following on social media platforms. By working with influencers to create and promote content, a website can expand its reach, increase engagement, and gain more backlinks.

In summary, off-page optimization strategies are just as important as on-page strategies when it comes to improving a website's search engine ranking. Through high-quality backlinks, social media marketing, guest blogging, influencer outreach, and other promotional activities, a website can enhance its online reputation, expand its reach, and ultimately achieve its goals.

Technical SEO

Technical SEO refers to optimizing the technical aspects of your website that can impact your search engine rankings. This includes things like:

- Importance of website speed and loading times

- Mobile optimization

- URL canonicalization

- Sitemap creation and submission

- Robots.txt file

- SSL certificate and website security

Technical SEO covers the strategies and techniques used to optimize the technical elements of a website to improve its search engine visibility. Technical SEO involves optimizing the backend of a website to make it more accessible to search engines and thus improve its overall ranking on search engine results pages (SERPs).

Here are some important technical SEO considerations to help ensure your website is optimized:

- **Site Speed:** Site speed refers to the time it takes for a page to load completely. Google has stated that site speed is a ranking factor, and sites that load faster are likely to rank higher than those that load slower. To improve site speed, consider things like optimizing images, minimizing redirects, compressing files, and using a Content Delivery Network (CDN).

- **Mobile Friendliness:** With a majority of internet users accessing websites on their mobile devices, it's essential to have a mobile-friendly website. A mobile-friendly website means a responsive design that adjusts according to the screen size of the device. Mobile-friendly websites are necessary for smooth user experience as well as improve search engine rankings, as Google considers mobile-friendliness as a ranking factor. You may see this function referred to as "responsive" design.

- **Site architecture:** A well-organized site architecture is essential for search engines to understand your website's content. A logical hierarchy, a sitemap, and easily navigable pages enhance your website's usability, which can improve user engagement and search engine rankings. Make use of heading tags (H1, H2, H3), schema markup, and structured data to communicate with search engines efficiently.

- **Site security:** The security of your website is crucial in the current online environment. Sites with HTTPS encryption are considered secure by Google and earn a slight ranking boost compared to unsecured sites. SSL certificates encrypt data sent between the server and the client, preventing malicious attacks. There is a variety of SSL certificates available, and LetsEncrypt, which is available at no cost. Unless you are handling secure data like credit cards, you may not need anything more than the free SSL option. Make sure your host directs the HTTP to the HTTPS directory of your website, as well as the www and non-www.

- **Indexability:** Search engines need to crawl and index your website to show it on search results pages. If search engines cannot crawl your website, your pages may not appear in search results. Check the crawlability of your website through the robots.txt file, the sitemap, and redirects.

- **URL Structures:** A well-structured URL that describes a web page's content makes it easier for users and search engines to understand that page's purpose. It's best to have a concise, descriptive, and hierarchical URL structure with targeted keywords that describe the content of the page.

Technical SEO is essential to optimize the backend of your website to improve its search engine visibility. While addressing technical aspects may seem daunting at first, it can yield worthwhile benefits in the form of higher search engine rankings, increased traffic, and better usability for your target audience.

WordPress Plugins for SEO

Overview of popular SEO plugins (Yoast SEO, All in One SEO, Jetpack, etc.)

SEO plugins are **extension modules for content management systems, browsers, and software solutions**. An SEO plugin expands the scope of the source software with special tasks and functions which affect search engine optimization, web analysis, online marketing, and other aspects.

There are a variety of plugins available to help you optimize your website for search engines. Here are some of the top plugins to consider:

- **All in One SEO Pack:** All in One SEO for WordPress is the original WordPress SEO plugin started in 2007. Over 3 million smart website owners use AIOSEO to properly setup WordPress SEO, so their websites can rank higher in search engines This plugin also offers a variety of tools to help you optimize your content for search engines, including XML sitemap creation, social integration, and automatic optimization of post titles and meta tags.

- **Rank Math:** Rank Math helps you set up title tags and meta descriptions on your pages. It can also create a robots.txt file and sitemap, both of which are important to control search engines' crawling behavior on your website.

- **Yoast SEO:** Yoast is one of the most popular SEO plugins for WordPress. It offers a variety of tools to help you optimize your content for search engines, including a snippet preview tool, XML sitemap creation, and more. Yoast also offers premium versions of their plugin, which offer additional features like keyword optimization and social integration.

- **SEO Ultimate:** SEO Ultimate is a full-featured SEO plugin that offers a variety of tools to help you optimize your website. Some of its features include the ability to edit your robots.txt file, create rich snippets, and optimize your site's link structure.

- **W3 Total Cache:** While not specifically an SEO plugin, W3 Total Cache can still be useful in improving your site's search engine rankings. This plugin helps to improve your site's load time, which can have a positive impact on your search engine rankings.

- **Broken Link Checker:** Broken links can harm your SEO efforts, so it's important to find and fix them quickly. This plugin will crawl your website and detect any broken links, making it easy for you to find and fix them.

There are other SEO plugins which can be found by searching SEO in the Plugins section of WordPress. To avoid serious problems, however, be sure that the plugin you select is tested with your version of WordPress. By utilizing SEO plugin tools you can maximize your website's visibility and attract more organic traffic.

Analyzing and Measuring SEO Results

Google Analytics – Google Search Console and other SEO tools and platforms; understanding website traffic metrics and performance indicators

After implementing an SEO strategy, it is crucial to measure the success of the efforts. This section will cover the essential steps to analyze and measure SEO results.

- Identify Key Performance Indicators (KPIs)

- To measure SEO success, it is crucial to determine the KPIs that will be used. These can include rankings, traffic, conversions, and revenue. Identifying KPIs early on will also help determine the success or failure of the SEO strategy.

- Set Baseline Metrics: Before any changes or optimizations are made, it is vital to establish baseline metrics. These metrics will serve as a comparison to measure the success of future SEO efforts.

- Track Progress and Measure Results: To track progress, it is essential to continuously monitor the selected KPIs. This can be done through analytics tools such as Google Analytics or SEMRush. Tracking progress will allow for the adjustment and optimization of SEO strategies to improve success.

- Analyze Data and Adjust Strategy: Analyzing data collected from tracking will allow for insights into how the SEO strategy is performing. This analysis can determine which areas need improvement and allow for adjustments to be made to the strategy.

- Report Results and Communicate with Stakeholders: Reporting results to stakeholders is an important aspect of measuring and analyzing SEO results. Communication with stakeholders will allow for the team to evaluate performance, make improvements, and align the SEO strategy with overall business goals.

In summary, analyzing and measuring SEO results is critical to the success of SEO efforts. By identifying KPIs, setting baseline metrics, tracking progress, analyzing data, making adjustments to strategies, and reporting results, businesses can improve their SEO success, increase traffic, and drive revenue.

SEO Best Practices and Future Trends

Next, we explored various best practices that can help improve your website's search engine rankings. From performing thorough keyword research to creating high-quality content, each step outlined in this guide can make a significant impact on your SEO success.

Key Takeaways

- Keyword research is critical to understanding your audience and what they are searching for online.

- Creating high-quality content that meets user intent is crucial to achieving long-term SEO success.

- Technical SEO, like optimizing website speed and mobile responsiveness, can improve your website's user experience and search engine rankings.

- Building backlinks from authoritative websites can boost your website's authority and improve search engine rankings.

Future Trends in SEO

As search engines continually evolve, SEO trends also shift. Some of the future SEO trends to keep an eye on include:

- Voice search optimization: As more people rely on digital assistants like Siri and Alexa, optimizing your website for voice search will become increasingly essential.

- Artificial intelligence: Search engines are using AI to better understand user behavior and deliver more relevant search results.

- Video SEO: With the rise of video content, optimizing your videos for search engines will become necessary.

Call to Action for Website Owners and Developers

To improve your website's SEO, consider implementing the following practices:

- Perform thorough keyword research to better understand your audience's search behavior.

- Create high-quality, user-focused content that meets their search intent.

- Optimize your website for speed and mobile responsiveness.

- Build high-quality backlinks to boost your website's authority.

Additional Resources for learning and staying up-to-date with SEO:

SEO is a constantly evolving field, so staying up-to-date is essential to maintaining your website's search engine rankings. Some additional resources to consider include:

- Moz Blog: This blog provides in-depth insights into SEO best practices.

- Search Engine Land: This website covers the latest news and trends in SEO and digital marketing.

- Google Webmaster Central: This resource provides information and tools to help website owners and developers improve their website's search engine rankings.

Chapter 14

WordPress Security

The security of your WordPress 6.x site is vital to protect your site from hackers and malicious attacks. In this chapter, we will guide you through several steps you can take to secure your WordPress 6.2 site using WordPress Admin security, server security, user security, plugin, and theme security.

WordPress is a popular platform used by millions of websites across the internet. Due to its ease of use and flexibility, WordPress is constantly evolving to meet the needs of its users. However, with great popularity comes a greater risk of cyber attacks and security breaches. To hackers, WordPress makes a big and attractive target.

WordPress 6.x has taken security to the next level by introducing new security features and enhancements. These features are designed to keep websites secure and prevent unauthorized access.

One of the most notable security plugins for WordPress is *WordFence*. WordFence is a powerful security tool that provides advanced security features for WordPress websites. It is designed to protect websites from various types of cyber attacks, including malware attacks, brute force attacks, and DDoS attacks. WordFence constantly monitors your website for any suspicious activities and sends alerts to the website admin. It also includes a firewall that blocks malicious traffic from entering your website. Additionally, WordFence provides two-factor authentication, login security, and website hardening capabilities.

In addition to WordFence, WordPress 6.x also includes several available built in enhanced security features. These features include automatic background updates, stronger password enforcement, and improved SSL support. These features make it easier for website owners to keep their websites secure and up-to-date.

It is crucial for website owners to keep WordPress secure by regularly updating plugins, themes, and the WordPress core. By using security plugins like WordFence and utilizing the built-in security features in WordPress , website owners can protect their websites from cyber attacks and ensure the safety of their users and visitors.

You will see examples of update notification (the red number dots) in the next chapter.

Chapter 15

What Could Go Wrong?

WordPress is a combination of many parts. One part, of course, is the WordPress, which is continually revised with new versions. At this writing, the current version is 6 appearing with a revision number between 6.0 and 6.9.

At times, it may seem like a three-ring circus. In Ring One, is WordPress. Appearing in Ring Two is the Theme, and finally in Ring Three are the performing Plugins.

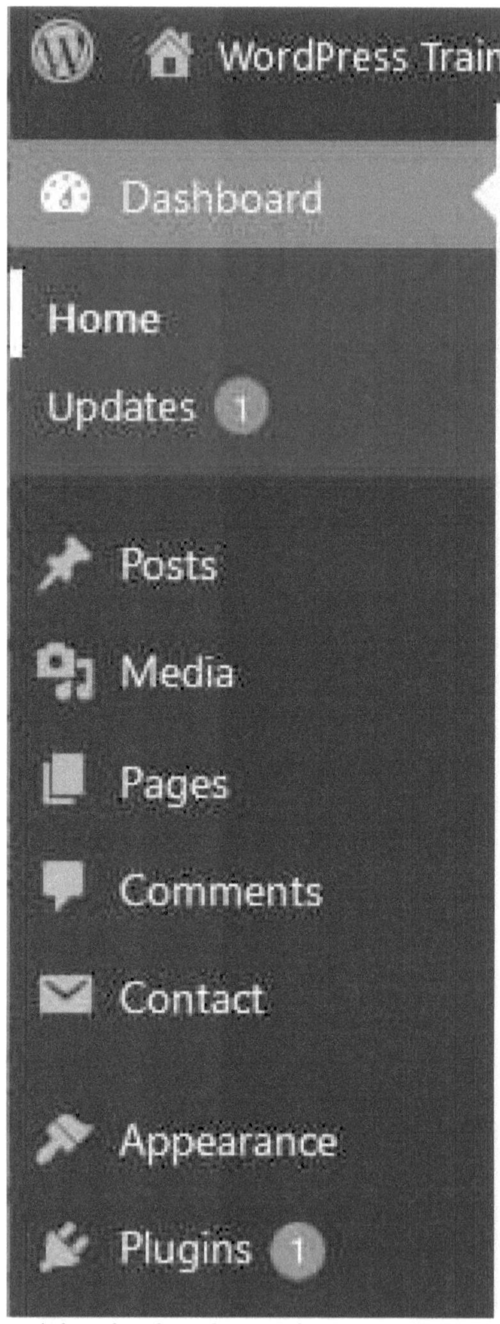

(The red circles indicate updates are available)

The Theme needs to be compatible with the installed WordPress version. Themes number in the thousands with a similar number of developers. Themes which are in active production are updated to match the current WordPress revision. A theme that is in active development will issue an update to remain compatible. Revisions and updates are not a problem unless the theme has been customized from the original, and still may remain compatible through many revisions. When an update is available, there is usually a notification in the top section of the WordPress administration Dashboard.

Plugins are also constantly being updated and revised. Like themes, each one has been created by any of several thousand developers. As with theme developers, themes frequently need to be changed to remain compatible with the WordPress and the currently selected theme.

The yellow alert in the example shows a new version is available. Also, note the third section of the screen to the right. It's a good idea to "Enable auto-updates".

There are other pieces of the puzzle to be aware of. If you have been around long enough, you will have experienced the changes in computer operating systems, whether Windows or Apple or even Linux. The same thing applies to WordPress. No, WordPress doesn't care what kind of computer you are using, it doesn't even care if you are accessing the dashboard from a laptop, a tablet, or a phone. Here, we are referring to the *programming language* of the *server* (or computer) where WordPress is hosted. The programming language is also subject to updates and revisions. That programming language is PHP.

At this writing, the current version of PHP is 8.x.x (The x stands for the series and revision number), but an older WordPress could be running on PHP 5.2.17, or 7.3.33 or some other version. Why does PHP change? Most times, the revisions are spurred by security issues that have arisen with the earlier versions. In others, the changes may be to enable new features. The PHP version is controlled by the hosting server, or the computer where WordPress is installed. Older versions of Themes, Plugins or WordPress may crash when PHP is updated. In that situation, an error message will appear in place of the website, indicating the need to contact the host. That's a good reason to have a regular schedule of backups.

What to do when something goes wrong? In most cases, the incompatibility problem is either with an outdated plugin or an incompatibility between plugins or even a conflict between the plugin and the WordPress core. Remember, these smaller PHP programs are developed independently by any of a thousand different programmers, focussed on just their own little piece of the WordPress kingdom.

In many cases, the server host technician will disable all the plugins and then enable them one at a time to discover the cause of the conflict

Sometimes, the hosting server has updated PHP to fend off a potential security threat and an outdated plugin will cause the website to crash. When it happens, contact technical support for the hosting server. That's when you need a good friend on the server end.

The solution is a process of elimination. If there has been a recent change in the PHP version, the host will simply dial back to the previous "outdated" PHP version. With an incompatible plugin, the support will disable all the installed plugins, and then turn them back on one by one, checking (refreshing) the website for each change until the "guilty" plugin is identified. Sometimes, it may be necessary to wait for the developer of that plugin to "catch up" in a few days, or it may be time to select another plugin for that function. For example, if a contact form plugin is the problem, you may decide to disable it, uninstall it, and then select, install, and setup another contact form plugin alternative.

Responsive Design

A word you will encounter in relation to any website is "Responsive". Visitors may view a website on any device, from a 36 inch computer screen to a laptop to a tablet to a smart phone. In the last two cases, they may view the screen vertically (Portrait mode) or horizontally (Landscape mode). They expect the website to "respond" to whatever device they choose to view it on. The website must adapt or "respond" the viewing device. For example, the text needs to be a consistent size and readable. The images need to scale to fit the screen. The arrangement of screen elements must change accordingly. That is something WordPress is particularly good at... MOST of the time. That's why it's important to view your finished website on multiple devices. As a shortcut, you can open the website in your computer, click F11 (PC) to switch off of full screen, then mouse over the right border and the cursor will change to double arrows. Click and drag the side, making the screen smaller and watch as the elements of the screen move and adjust to different widths. If there are problems, they will most likely be with the content of columns or tables. Make adjustments to solve any problems you discover.

By the way, here's a tip: Try to limit your main menu to 7 items. Having more than 7 menu items (tabs) or long menu titles will cause the menu to "spill" over to a second line on devices with smaller display areas. If you need more menu titles, simply add them as drop-down menu tabs. Go to Appearance, Menus and add the tabs you need. Click and drag the new menu item to the location where you want it and shift it slightly to the right. It will appear like a stair step. You have just created a drop-down menu item.

Don't forget to "save" your menu. Be careful NOT to click the "delete" button or you will need to create your menu all over again.

Chapter 16

Conclusion

WordPress 6.x is an excellent platform for anyone looking to create a website with no coding knowledge required. This book has introduced you to various features of WordPress 6.x, including installation, navigation, the WordPress editor, themes, plugins, optimization, security, and user management. With this ebook, you have the basic knowledge to create and manage a successful WordPress 6.x website.

WordPress is a powerful content management system that has revolutionized the online publishing industry. It provides features that simplify website creation and management, making it accessible to businesses, organizations, and individuals across the world. The platform has evolved to improve user experience, security, and scalability, making it the most popular website builder in the world.

A key aspect of WordPress is its open-source nature. The development community has contributed thousands of plugins and themes that make it possible for users to create just about any type of website they can imagine. Its commitment to accessibility and inclusivity has made it an ideal choice for website owners who want to ensure that their sites are available to all users, regardless of their abilities.

WordPress is the king, dominating almost half the internet (43%). For Content Management, that dominance soars to over 64%. Other competitors to WordPress in the Content Management sphere include Atlassian Cloud, Joomla!, My Salesforce and Drupal. Of these, Drupal most resembles the functionality of WordPress, with a database core and interchangeable design themes.

Here's a comparison:

1. Complexity and Learning Curve:

- Atlassian Cloud: Atlassian products, such as Jira and Confluence, have a steeper learning curve compared to WordPress, especially if you are new to project management or collaboration tools.

- My Salesforce: Salesforce is a comprehensive CRM platform with extensive features and customization options. It can be overwhelming for beginners because of its complexity.

- Drupal: Drupal is a powerful content management system (CMS), but it has a higher learning curve compared to WordPress. It requires more technical knowledge and coding skills to set up and customize.

2. Cost:

- Atlassian Cloud: Atlassian Cloud offers a range of pricing plans, and while they have a free tier, the more advanced features and functionality come with higher costs, which may not fit into a beginner's budget.

- Salesforce: Salesforce is known for being an enterprise-level CRM platform, and the pricing reflects that. The costs associated with Salesforce can be quite high, making it less budget-friendly for beginners. For major corporations, government, manufacturing, technology and large retail, healthcare and financial services with huge sites and millions of users, it's a common choice. Salesforce is also used by colleges and national nonprofits.

- Drupal: Drupal itself is an open-source CMS, which means it's free to use. However, you may incur costs for hosting, themes, modules, and professional support, especially if you require additional features beyond the core functionality.

3. Customization and Flexibility:

- Atlassian Cloud: While Atlassian Cloud products offer various customization options, they are primarily designed for specific use cases such as project management or collaboration. It may be challenging to extend their functionality beyond their intended purpose.

- My Salesforce: Salesforce is highly customizable, but this flexibility often requires a deeper understanding of the platform and coding skills. Beginners may find it overwhelming to tailor Salesforce to their specific needs.

- Drupal: Drupal is known for its flexibility and extensibility. It allows you to create highly customized websites or web applications. However, achieving this level of customization often requires technical expertise, making it less beginner-friendly.

4. Community and Support:

- Atlassian Cloud: Atlassian has an active user community and provides documentation and support resources. However, as a beginner, you may find it more challenging to access the level of support available compared to WordPress, which has a larger and more beginner-friendly community.

- My Salesforce: Salesforce has a vast community and extensive documentation, but it primarily caters to enterprise users. Finding beginner-friendly resources or support may be more difficult compared to WordPress.

- Drupal: Drupal has an active community, but it is relatively smaller compared to WordPress. It may be more challenging to find beginner-friendly resources or get support, especially if you encounter issues or have specific questions.

5. Overall, WordPress is often considered more beginner-friendly and budget-friendly compared to Atlassian Cloud, My Salesforce, and Drupal. It has a large user community, extensive documentation, and a wide range of free and affordable themes and plugins. However, the choice ultimately depends on your specific requirements, goals, and willingness to invest time and effort in learning a new platform.

What about GoDaddy Site Builder? Again, a proprietary (restricted) system. If you like GoDaddy, it's no problem. If you don't and you want to move, you will be forced to start over. Just for fun, try a Google or Bing search for "I hate GoDaddy" and see what you find.

Then there is Joomla! In 2011, Joomla! had a peak market share of 10.9%, but has since decreased to around 2.4-2.5% of the Content Management System market.

What about oher smaller competitors, like WIX? WIX occupies less than 1% of the market. The main disadvantages of Wix are its lack of fully responsive templates and it doesn't let you switch templates once you've selected one. WIX lacks responsive design. We've already discussed the importance of responsive design in the previous chapter. Responsiveness is the ability for a website design to adjust to different display modes, from computer monitor to tablet to smart phones.

WIX websites are often hosted on a sub-domain of wix.com, which means there is no cost for domain registration, but at the same time, the user does not have their own online identity. WIX is also proprietary. There is no switching to a different Wix hosting server if there is something you don't like. It comes down to starting over with another alternative. Contrast that with WordPress that can be easily transported to other WordPress hosting servers. There's even a plugin to do that.

WIX will claim that WordPress is more costly. While there are options for upgraded themes and plugins, those are the very things that provide expanding the functionality of a website. Wix offers a range of pricing plans, including a free plan with basic features and advertisements. Paid plans provide access to more advanced features, custom domains, and the ability to remove ads.

Shopify advertisements include a fictional example of a person who says they "added one thing and the whole website crashed", possibly implying WordPress. That never happens with WordPress. If you make a mistake in WordPress, simply go back and change it. Shopify is a structure specifically to be a simplified shopping cart site. Its capability is limited to that function. If that's all you need, then go for it. If you need more, then WordPress provides you with the tools you need. Again, Shopify is a separate environment and there is no "moving" to another provider other than starting over. Shopify advertises its ability to display on mobile devices. WordPress is also fully and automatically "responsive" on mobile devices, as are almost all the other choices.

If you intend to extend your marketing capabilities by including a blog in your ecommerce website, the logical solution is WordPress and WooCommerce. Just be sure to update your blog on a consistent basis. The latest blog post that is two years old does not encourage people to sign up for your newsletter.

By the way, MailChimp and similar services provide ability to automate the process of sending newsletters automatically whenever you add a new post to your blog or at a scheduled time. It can represent a significant advantage to your marketing effort.

Where do you go from here?

Once you have a basic understanding of the WordPress platform, you can venture into the next level with developer tools like Elementor, which offers an upgrade that employs Artificial Intelligence. DIVI, a drag-and-drop design platform that is less expensive than Elementor, but it has a steep learning curve and is probably not a good choice for beginners. Some WordPress developers design themes around the features provided by these plugin tools.

Here are some of the most popular WordPress builder plugin tools:

- Elementor (www.Elementor.com)

- Divi Builder (www.ElegantThemes.com)

- SeedProd (www.SeedProd.com)

- Beaver Builder (www.WPBeaverBuilder.com)

- WP Bakery Page Builder (www.WPBakery.com)

- Brizy Builder (www.brizy.io)

These builder tools are commonly found in paid WordPress themes available from sources such as ThemeForest.net, TemplateMonster.com, MyThemeShop, Elegant-Thmes, Mojo Marketplace, and others.

There are two cautions to note:

One: Using these will require getting used to different ways to access and edit content.

Two: Very often, these plugins will require paid renewal after an initial period such as one year. While a developer might license up to 50 websites for a cost under $200, your annual renewal cost for a single website might be $89.

When purchasing a paid WordPress theme be sure to note what plugins are required and take into account the ongoing cost after the initial installation. Be sure to include that cost in your annual hosting budget. An outdated plugin can mean your site cannot be updated to keep up with PHP revisions, which leaves you more vulnerable to attack.

WordPress is a vital platform that continues to grow and evolve. Its commitment to open-source development and inclusivity has ensured that it will remain a prominent player in the web development industry for years to come.

If you enjoyed this book, please take a few moments to write a lovely review where you purchased it and recommend it to your friends and social media followers!

Please review!

If you enjoyed this book, please take a few moments to write a nice review where you purchased it and recommend it to your friends and social media followers! You can also find a review form on my website at TimTrottWrites.com

About the Author

Tim Trott's writing style might be similar to that of Isaac Asimov, or Aldous Huxley and perhaps Philip K. Dick, or Ray Bradbury. Of course! Tim grew up reading Asimov and Huxley, along with Franklin .W. Dixon (*Hardy Boys*). Those authors were bound to have an influence.

His fiction writing combines elements of psychological thriller, science, and speculative fiction. The narrative style is engaging, with a focus on character experiences and internal conflicts, which draws the reader into the protagonist's psychological journey. If you look closely, you may find an underlying narrative.

He is a writer who is passionate about investigation and shedding light on important issues. Tim Trott's writing, whether fiction or non-fiction, demonstrates a commitment to research and an adeptness in communicating complex topics with clarity, skills honed during his early career in broadcasting.

A lifelong student and observer of current events and issues, Tim brings a wealth of perspective and insight into his work. Despite not being a well-known author, his writing holds value because of the information he provides and the quality of his communication. His writing is a testament to a lifetime spent in diverse occupations, each contributing to a tapestry of perspectives on the complex issues shaping our world.

Research informs Tim Trott's writing. His exploration of this multifaceted topic goes beyond the headlines, delving into the nuances that often escape casual observation. Drawing on the skills cultivated throughout his career, Tim navigates the subject's complexities with a balanced and informed perspective.

Beyond the mere presentation of facts, Tim's writing reflects a commitment to fostering understanding and informed dialogue. His ability to distill intricate information into accessible narratives makes his work informative and engaging for readers from all walks of life.

In his post-retirement years, Tim Trott has found a renewed purpose in contributing to the discourse surrounding critical societal issues. Through his writing, he continues to share his wealth of knowledge, providing readers with the tools they need to form well-informed opinions on the pressing matters of our time.

Member: Florida Writers Association (FWA) and Florida Authors and Publishers Association (FAPA).

Tim Trott invites you to visit his website at TimTrottWrites.com.

Please consider these other books by the author:

Science Fiction/Paranormal:

- *What If... (Vol 1),*

- *What If... (Vol 2),*

- *The Brown Bean Coffee Shoppe (Book one)*

Biography:

- *Out of the Blue: The Life and Legend of Kirby "Sky King" Grant,*

- *First Through the Fire (the story of Talbert Gray)*

Education:

- *Understanding WordPress 6.x for Beginners,*

- *FAA UAG 107 Remote Pilot Study Guide,*

- *Drone Operations*

Security:

- *Guarding Against Online Identity Theft*

- *Proteccion de Identidad*

Politics/History:

- *T is for Treason, Broken Border,*

- *Party of NO,*

- *Trumped*

Misc/LCB:

- *LOTTO TRAKR*